WHO IS THIS CHILD?

From Common Babe
to King *of* Kings

JOHN ORTBERG

ZONDERVAN®

ZONDERVAN.com/
AUTHORTRACKER
follow your favorite authors

ZONDERVAN

Who Is this Child?
Copyright © 2012 by John Ortberg

This title is also available as a Zondervan ebook.
Visit www.zondervan.com/ebooks.

Requests for information should be addressed to:

Zondervan, *Grand Rapids, Michigan* 49530

ISBN 978-0-310-32688-5

Cover design: *Extra Credit Projects*
Cover photography: *Jupiter Images*®
Interior design: *Beth Shagene*

Printed in the United States of America

12 13 14 15 16 /DPM/ 12 11 10 9 8 7 6 5 4 3 2 1

Contents

The Mother. 5

The Child 15

Sources. 45

The Mother

———•••———

Before we get into the story of the one who comes at Christmas, and who he really was, I want to take you into a prelude—a prelude that is the story about the one person who knew him best: Mary, his mother. Mary's story is about a song she sang, before the Christmas night, when Gabriel came to her in the sixth month of her pregnancy. The song shows that of all people, she "got it,"—what was about to happen. This is the lead-up to the Christmas event. And the two characters most in view were seen as being the least, with the least to give: a mother and a baby child.

So Mary composed the very first song ever inspired by the birth of Jesus. It is maybe the most influential song ever written. Maybe the most profound. It was written by a girl who was probably fifteen years old.

Yet the capacity of both her mind and spirit, and the amazing fact of the Son she carried and raised, means that Mary's song can change your attitude and mindset and life — on Christmas day or any other. But the song did not begin well.

When the angel Gabriel told Mary that she was going to have a child, this was *not* welcome news. She was engaged to Joseph but not married. She would be an unwed pregnant teenage girl. She did not know at that point how it would turn out.

Joseph could reject Mary. She could be subject to stoning; according to Torah, that's what was supposed to happen. For sure, as someone who was known to be pregnant before marriage, she would be the subject of rumors and gossip. If this child were in some sense to be the Messiah, there would be danger from other kings. And there was. Mary had to flee for her survival and begin married life in exile in Egypt. In a very real way, she suffered for the Messiah before the Messiah ever suffered for her.

But Mary sang her song. And she magnified God. She knew him to be the Mighty One. So she said to the angel, "Behold the Lord's servant. Let it be according to your word."

Mary went on to write the first song of Christmas, sometimes called the "Magnificat" because in Latin it starts with that word. As in,

> My soul glorifies the Lord
> and my spirit rejoices in God my
> Savior.

———•◆•———

In Mary's day, the most important man in the world was Caesar Augustus. He had been adopted by Julius Caesar. After Julius Caesar died, Augustus was declared to be divine, so he was given the title "Son of God." When Augustus seized power, he ended the civil wars (you might remember Antony and Cleopatra); so he brought peace—*Pax Romana*. Because of this, he was called the peoples' Savior, or *Soter*. The inauguration of Augustus as emperor was declared throughout the empire as "good news"—the same term from which we get "gospel."

Notice that Rome would use four expressions to describe Augustus:

> *Savior*
> *Son of God*
> *Bringer of peace*
> Announcement of his reign as the
> *Gospel/Good News*

But Mary alone understood who Caesar was and who her son was.

There are all these characters in the story: Joseph, Wise Men, Herod, shepherds, Elizabeth, Zechariah the priest.... One person gets it. One person figures out who Jesus is. The very first identifier and proclaimer of the Good News, the Gospel of Jesus, is an unwed, maybe fifteen-year-old girl: Mary the theologian.

Without dismissing the important role played by apostles or evangelists themselves, we must remember the story now being recorded in the gospels began when Mary began to ponder, and, after pondering, when Mary began to tell the story about Jesus to others.

———•◆•———

What song do you sing, at Christmas time or any other time? We are marked by the songs we hear.

We are marked by the songs we hear from the people in our lives.

We are marked by the songs we hear from the people in our lives. Sometimes, if I hear a song often enough, I start to sing it too. Your song becomes our song. Mary had a song. How it must have pleased the heart of the Father when he thought this was the song his Son would hear. She must have sung it to Jesus all the time.

What's amazing is to look at how in so many ways Jesus is Mary's song come to life. She would have told him how Gabriel said to her, "Nothing is impossible with God."

And it isn't; Jesus proved that.

Jesus would begin the single most compelling speech in history, the Sermon on the Mount, by telling people in humble states, "Blessed are the poor in spirit;... blessed are those who mourn;... blessed are the meek" — because through Jesus the kingdom of God has come to you.

One of the central characteristics of Jesus' teaching about kingdom life is sometimes called the Great Inversion: the first shall be last; the least shall be greatest; those who give up their life will receive it.

The Great Inversion may be the central theme of Mary's song: the humble will be lifted up; the rulers and the rich who exalt themselves will be humbled.

Mary would have sung her song to little Jesus: "He has filled the hungry with good things."

Notice to this day that at Christmastime there will be Santa Clauses ringing bells at shopping malls to collect money. Jesus' birth is the primary time of year that people's hearts turn to give; that's the song we sing.

We can imagine how many times Mary said to that little boy: "Your heavenly Father has always been faithful. If he ever asks you to do a hard thing, Son, remember how your life started. Remember what your mom said when she was a scared young unmarried teenage girl."

Years later, in the garden, in the shadow of the Cross, the Father did ask his Son to do a hard thing: To take onto himself the weight of the sins of the world — yours and mine — so that forgiveness and love could begin the Great Reversal. And the Son said, "Not my will. Yours be done."

He was God of very God.

He was also his mother's son.

Mary's life is a prelude to his.

The Child

—·◆·—

He entered the world with no dignity.

He would have been known as a *mamzer*, a child whose parents were not married. All languages have a word for *mamzer*, and all of them are ugly. His cradle was a feeding trough. His nursery mates had four legs. He was wrapped in rags. He was born in a cave, targeted for death, raised on the run.

He would die with even less dignity: convicted, beaten, bleeding, abandoned, naked, shamed. He had no status. Dignity on the level of a king is the last word you would associate with Jesus.

There is a king in the story, however. Jesus was born "during the time of King Herod."

To an ancient reader, Herod — not Jesus — would have been the picture of greatness. Born of noble birth, leader of armies, Herod was so highly regarded by the Roman Senate that they gave him the title "King of the Jews" when he was only thirty-three years old. He was so politically skilled that he held on to his throne for forty years, even persuading Caesar Augustus to retain him after he had backed Caesar's mortal enemy, Mark Antony. He was the greatest builder of his day. "No one in Herod's period built so extensively with projects that shed such a bright light on that world." The massive stones of the temple he built are visible two thousand years later.

Jesus was a builder. A carpenter. He likely did construction in a town called Sepphoris for one of Herod's sons. Nothing he built is known to have endured.

In the ancient world, all sympathies would have rested with Herod. He was nearer to the gods, guardian of the *Pax Romana*, adviser to Caesar. The definitive biography of him is called: *Herod: King of the Jews, Friend of the Romans.* The two phrases are connected: if Herod were not a friend of the Romans, he would not be king of the Jews.

Jesus would be called "friend of sinners." It was not a compliment. He would be arrested as an enemy of the Romans.

Herod ruled in a time when only the ruthless survived. He cowered before no one. He had ten or eleven wives. He suspected the ambitions of the only one he ever truly loved, so he had her executed. He also had his mother-in-law, two of his brothers-in-law, and two of his own sons by his favorite wife executed. When his old barber tried to stick up for his sons, he had his barber executed. Caesar remarked that (given the Jewish refusal to eat pork) it was better to be Herod's pig than his son. Herod rewarded his friends and punished his enemies, the sign of a great-souled man in his day.

Jesus, when he was a man, would be nearly as silent and passive before Herod's successor as he was when he was a baby before Herod.

Herod clung to his title to the end. While he was dying, he had a group of protestors arrested, the ringleaders burned alive, and the rest executed. Five days before his death, he had another son executed for trying to grab power prematurely. His will instructed scores of prominent Israelites be executed on the day he died so there would be weeping in Israel.

Herod was considered by Rome the most effective ruler over Israel the empire ever had. No one would bear that title "King of the Jews" again, except for a crucifixion victim impaled for a few hours one Friday afternoon years later.

No one would bear that title "King of the Jews" after Herod, except for a crucifixion victim impaled one Friday afternoon years later.

We are used to thinking of Herod as the cardboard villain of the Christmas pageant, but he would have been considered great by many in his day, especially those whose opinion would have mattered most. How greatness came to look different to the world is part of what this story is about. No one knew it yet, but an ancient system of Dignity was about to collapse. Human dignity itself would descend from its Herod-protecting perch and go universal.

The lives of Herod and Jesus intersected when magi from the East asked where they could find the one born (notice the title) "king of the Jews." Herod claimed to follow the religion of Israel, but it was the pagan magi who sought truth with respect and humility. There is something about this Jesus, even on his first day, that had a way of forcing people to declare where they stand.

"When King Herod heard this he was disturbed" (major understatement here), "... and all Jerusalem with him." Now it's clear why.

Herod "was furious, and he gave orders to kill all the boys in Bethlehem and its vicinity who were two years old and under ... Then what was said through the prophet Jeremiah was fulfilled: 'A voice is heard in Ramah, weeping and great mourning, Rachel weeping for her children and refusing to be comforted, because they are no more.'"

I grew up in a church that did Christmas pageants every year. We would dress up in bathrobes and pretend to be Joseph and Mary and the shepherds and the wise men. Somehow that Herodian part of the story never made it into those pageants. It became known as the *slaughter of the innocents.*

This is not the kind of story you would write songs about. The night Jesus is born, all is not calm, all is not bright. That little baby does not "sleep in heavenly peace."

Herod sends soldiers to Bethlehem into the homes of peasant families who are powerless to stop them. They break in, and when they find an infant boy, they take out a sword and plunge it into that baby's body. Then they leave. Someone wrote a song centuries later: "O little town of Bethlehem, how still we see thee lie." Bethlehem was not still when Herod came for Jesus.

Matthew underlined the pain of the gap between peasant and king: *"Rachel weeping for her children."* The rabbis said that centuries earlier, the Jewish matriarch Rachel had been buried in Bethlehem near the major road leading out of Israel so that she could weep for the helpless exiles leaving their home.

——•◆•——

Soon some more people would leave. Jesus' parents would flee to Egypt. Meanwhile, Jesus lay helpless and unaware. Herod, who built cities and ruled armies, was called Herod the Great.

No one called Jesus "the Great." Jesus is repeatedly given a different title by Matthew: "'Go and search carefully for *the child*' ... the place where *the child* was ... they saw *the child* with his mother ... 'take *the child* ... and escape to Egypt' ... 'take *the child* ... and go to the land of Israel' ... so he got up, took *the child*."

The title "child," especially in that day, would be a vivid contrast with "king" or "great." In the ancient, status-ordered world, children were at the bottom of the ladder. In both Greek and Latin, the words for children meant "not speaking"; children lacked the dignity of reason.

Plato wrote about the "mob of motley appetites pains and pleasures" one would find in children, along with slaves and women. Children were noted for fear, weakness, and helplessness. "None among all the animals is so prone to tears," wrote Pliny the Elder. To be a child was to be dependent, defenseless, fragile, vulnerable, at risk.

Those were not qualities associated with heroism in the ancient world. A hero was someone who made things happen. A child was someone things happened to. In old stories about Hercules, he grabbed two poisonous snakes while he was still in the cradle and killed them with his bare, chubby little hands. By the second and third century AD, people made up stories about Jesus having great power as a child: in one of them he makes clay birds come alive, in another he magically causes the death of a child. But they are the kind of stories the Greeks made up to give their heroes dignity as children. The four Gospels have no stories like this about Jesus as a child.

Herod the Great made things happen. Things happened to the child Jesus.

———•◆•———

There is a reversal going on in this story. The next season of Jesus' life is introduced with the phrase "After Herod died...."

In fact, three times in chapter 2 alone, Matthew mentions the fact that Herod is dead. Matthew wants the reader to know: Herod the Great, with all his wealth, glory, power, and crown, is now Herod the Dead.

Herod died. This is a subtle reminder of a great leveler. Who else is going to die?

Herod died. This is a subtle reminder of a great leveler. Who else is going to die?

A friend of mine gave me a watch I still wear. One hand says *Remember*, and the other hand says *You will die*. Every time somebody asks me, "What time is it?" I look at this watch. Every time I look at my wrist, what I see is, "Remember you will die." A *friend* gave me this watch. Not a good friend really ... but it helps me remember.

A new time had come with Jesus, a time when thinking about kings and children would begin to shift. You might say there was an idea lying there in the manger along with a baby. An idea that had mostly been confined to a little country called Israel, but which was waiting for the right time to crawl out into the wider world — an idea which that wider world would be unable to wholly resist.

All peoples in the ancient world had gods. Their gods had different names, but what they shared was a hierarchal way of ordering life. At the top of creation were the gods; under them was the king. Under the king were members of the court and the priests, who reported to the king. Below them were artisans, merchants, and craftspeople, and below them was a large group of peasants and slaves — the dregs of humanity.

The king was divine, or semi-divine. The king was understood to be made in the image of the god who created him. Only the king was made in the image of the god. This was a dividing line between the king and the rest of the human race. Peasants and slaves were not made in the image of *the* god; they were created by inferior gods.

This is the Dignity Gap. The farther down the ladder, the wider the gap.

But that gap was challenged by an idea that lay there in the manger, an idea that had been guarded by Israel for centuries: *There is one God. He is good. And every human being has been made in his image.*

Because God is Creator of all, the earth is full of creatures. But human beings reflect the image of God in a way no other creature can, with the capacity to reason, choose, communicate, and invent. Man is a critter who can Twitter.

Imagine what it did to the hearts of the dregs of humanity to be told that not just the king but they too were created in the image of the one great God. Male and female, slaves and peasants, made in God's image.

God said that these human beings are to exercise "dominion." That's a royal word, but it is no longer reserved for the few. Every human being has royal dignity. When Jesus looked at people, he saw the image of God. He saw this in everyone. It caused him to treat each person with dignity. This is the idea to which that little baby in a manger was heir, which had been given to Israel, which would be clarified and incarnated in his life in a way not seen before.

———•◆•———

The belief that all people are made in God's image has woven its way into our world in a manner we often do not see. The United States' Declaration of Independence begins, "We hold these truths to be self-evident: That all men are created equal; that they are endowed by their Creator with certain inalienable rights;

that among these rights are life, liberty, and the pursuit of happiness."

There is a raft of ideas here: that people are created, not accidents; that their Creator gives them certain endowments and confers worth on them. This worth means that they come with certain rights that ought to be respected for a society to be considered good. This is true for all human beings — *all* are created equal.

The idea of the equality of all human beings was not "self-evident" to the ancient world. Aristotle did not think all men were created equal. He wrote that inequality — masters and slavery — was the natural order of things: "For that some should rule and others be ruled is a thing not only necessary, but expedient; from the hour of their birth, some are marked out for subjection, others for rule."

Who came in between Aristotle and Thomas Jefferson to change this?

Yale philosopher Nicholas Wolterstorff observes that throughout world history, human beings by nature tend to be tribal. We don't think of "outsiders" as having the same worth or rights. What accounts for the emergence of this moral subculture that says *every* human being has rights?

Wolterstorff gives an amazing answer: the teaching of the Scriptures, clarified and made available to all the world through Jesus, that every human being is made in the image of God, and loved by God.

—•◆•—

There are gradations of talent, strength, intelligence, and beauty. Martin Luther King Jr. said, "There are no gradations of the image of God."

The reason every person has great worth, for Jesus, is that every person is loved by God. Each person has what might be called "bestowed worth."

> *The reason every person has great worth, for Jesus, is that every person is loved by God and has "bestowed worth."*

When one of our daughters was tiny, she had one doll that she loved above all others — a doll that initially belonged to her sister. She loved that doll so much, she commandeered her, and we had to buy her sister another one. She called her doll Baby Tweezers. That doll got loved so much that her dress fell apart, and all she had was her little plastic head and limbs and squishy soft inner body. She then was renamed "Naked Baby Tweezers." She was not loved for her beauty. She set a new standard for ugly. She was loved: "Because." Just "because."

We could never throw out Baby Tweezers. Our daughter loved Baby Tweezers — and we loved our daughter. Baby Tweezers has "bestowed worth."

We all know this kind of love: Get a pet, live in a house twenty years, raise your kids there. You come to love it — not because it's more excellent; just "because."

Novelist George MacDonald delighted in writing about princesses and princes. Someone asked him why he always wrote about princesses. "Because every girl is a princess," he said.

When the questioner was confused,

MacDonald asked what a princess is. "The daughter of a king," the man answered.

"Very well, then every little girl is a princess."

Every human being is the child of a King.

—·•·—

The ancient world did not teach this. Ordinary children did not share the king's image. They were not created by the same god. And so they grew up in a different world.

In the Roman Empire, some babies grew up to be women, who were generally shut off from education and public life. Some grew up to be slaves, who were needed for their labor but regarded as inferior to those who were free.

Many babies did not grow up at all. In the ancient world, unwanted children were often simply left to die, a practice called "exposure." The head of the household had the legal right to decide the life or death of other members of the family. This decision was usually made during the first eight or so days of life. (Plutarch wrote that until that time the child was "more like a plant than a human being.")

The most common reasons to expose a child would be if the family lived in poverty, or if a wealthy family did not want the estate divided up, or if the child was the wrong gender (meaning a girl), or if the child was illegitimate.

The Jews were opposed to exposure because of their faith. Since Jesus was regarded as a *mamzer* — the descendant of a forbidden relationship between two Jews — he would likely not have survived had Joseph been Roman. Abandoned children were often left on a dump or a dung hill. They most often died; sometimes they were rescued, but usually this was for becoming enslaved. This happened often enough that hundreds of ancient names are variations of the word *kopros*, which was Greek for "dung."

Babies that were disabled or appeared weak were often disposed of by drowning. An ancient Roman law said that a boy who was "strikingly deformed" had to be disposed of quickly. One archeological dig found "a gruesome discovery," the bones of "nearly 100 little babies apparently murdered and thrown into the sewer."

Ancient parents could be as tender and loving as moderns. But children had value to the extent that they could serve the state. And the state was embodied by Herod. In themselves, children were disposable.

Then the child born in Bethlehem grew up. He began to say things about children no one else thought of.

One day Jesus was asked the question, "Who ... is the greatest in the kingdom of heaven?" Matthew wrote: "He called a little child to him, and placed the child among them. [Maybe a child named *Kopros*.] And he said: '... Unless you change and become like little children, you will never enter the kingdom of heaven. Therefore, whoever takes the lowly position of this child is the greatest in the kingdom of heaven.'"

Jesus said it wasn't the child's job to become like Herod. Rather, it was Herod's job to become like the child. Greatness comes to people who die to appearing great. No one else in the ancient world—not even the rabbis—used children as an example of conversion.

> *Jesus said it wasn't the child's job to become like Herod. It was Herod's job to become like the child.*

Then Jesus said the kind of thing that would literally never enter the mind of another human being to say: "And whoever welcomes one such child in my name welcomes me."

Kopros has a new name.

There were many clubs and associations in the ancient world. None of the qualities associated with children—weakness, helplessness, lowliness—qualified one to join any of them. There were no clubs for children. Until Jesus.

Another time Jesus acted out a little parable of this teaching. Children "were brought" to Jesus. The language says they could not even come themselves: passive, dependent. The disciples rebuked the parents. Jesus rebuked the disciples. "Let the little children come to me, and do not hinder them, for the kingdom of heaven belongs to such as these."

A kingdom for children. Before Walt Disney. And the little children came.

As the movement that Jesus started spread, it created an alternative community for children. Early instructions among his followers, such as the *Didache* in the second century, prohibit the widespread practices of abortion, exposure, and infanticide.

There is an old joke that the most basic of the Ten Commandments for parents is "Thou shalt not kill." In some ways, that is a new joke; in the ancient world it was the basis of a revolution. Exposure was forbidden—not because the state needed more workers (Caesar Augustus would try to limit it on this basis), but because as the Shepherd of Hermas put it, "All babies are glorious before God." Saint Ambrose of Milan said that the church must care not only for babies, but also for the poor, because poverty often destroys their ability to care for children.

Homer did not say that Zeus or Apollo

or Pan valued all human beings equally. G. K. Chesterton wrote that the elevation of the dignity of childhood would have made no sense to the ancients. It came into the world through Jesus, and even where belief in him has eroded the elevation of childhood, Jesus' thought remains: "The pagan world, as such, would not have understood any such thing as a serious suggestion that a child is higher or holier than a man. It would have seemed like the suggestion that a tadpole is higher or holier than a frog. . . . Peter Pan does not belong to the world of Pan but the world of Peter."

An average life expectancy of thirty or so meant the ancient world was full of orphans. Now for the first time, a community began to collect money to care for them indiscriminately. At baptism children would receive "god parents," who would promise to care for them if their parents died.

By the late fourth century, a Christian emperor outlawed the practice of exposure for the entire empire. Over time, instead of leaving unwanted babies on a dung hill, people began to leave them outside a monastic community or a church. The beginnings of what would be known as orphanages began to rise, usually associated with monasteries or cathedrals.

Merely claiming a religious label is no more a guarantee of family health now than it was for Adam and Eve. But those who live in a culture truly touched and changed by Christianity view individuals differently because of Jesus, whatever they might think of him. The ordinary and the lowly have great dignity. All children should live. All human beings are created equal.

A few years ago I spoke at an event where the hero was a dad named Dick Hoyt. When Dick's son Richard was born, the umbilical cord was wrapped around his neck. He was brain-damaged; he would never be able to walk or speak. In ancient Rome, both by custom and by law, he would have had to be discarded.

Dick and his wife brought Richard home to care for him. When he was eleven, they took him to the engineering department at Tufts University to see if a device could be invented to help him communicate. They were told that his brain was incapable of comprehension.

"Tell him a joke," Dick said. When they did, Richard laughed. The department constructed a computer that allowed Richard to laboriously type out a sentence by hitting a button with the side of his head — the only part of his body he could move.

When Richard heard one day about a benefit race being run to help a young man who had been paralyzed, he typed out a sentence: *Dad, I want to run.* By this time Dick was forty, a self-described porker who had never run over a mile. He somehow pushed his son in a wheelchair over the course. Afterward, Richard wrote the sentence that changed Dick's life: *When I ran, I didn't feel disabled.* Dick then made running a pastime.

We watched videos of this strong father pushing and pulling and carrying his son over two hundred triathlons. Not a dry eye in the room. More than eighty-five times Dick has pushed Richard's wheelchair the 26.2 miles that make up a marathon. Dick's best time is a little over two and a half hours — within thirty minutes of the world's record, which was not set, as sports columnist Rick Reilly observed, by a guy pushing his son in a wheelchair.

I said earlier that the hero in the room was Dick. That's not quite right. Dick said that his hero — his inspiration, his courage, his reason for running — is the 110-pound motionless, speechless body of the man in the chair.

The Greeks loved physical excellence and perfection, the nobility of striving. They gave us the Olympics, through which mortals strove to be like the gods of Olympus. They gave us the marathon, the ultimate test of human will and strength. They did not give us the story of a marathon being run by a man carrying his crippled son.

I recently read an article that speaks of a "theology of disability," which explores how the divine is present in limitation

and suffering and handicap. It is a phrase
that would have been senseless in Rome.

———•◆•———

The child in Bethlehem would grow up
to be a friend of sinners, not a friend of
Rome. He would spend his life with the
ordinary and the unimpressive. He would
pay deep attention to lepers and cripples,
to the blind and the beggar, to prostitutes
and fishermen, to women and children.
He would announce the availability of a
kingdom different from Herod's, a kingdom where blessing — of full value and
worth with God — was now conferred on
the poor in spirit and the meek and the
persecuted.

People would not understand what all
this meant. We still do not.

*A revolution was starting — a slow,
quiet movement that began at the
bottom of society and would undermine
the pretensions of the Herods.*

But a revolution was starting — a slow,

quiet movement that began at the bottom of society and would undermine the pretensions of the Herods. It was a movement that was largely underground, like a cave around Bethlehem where a dangerous baby might be born and hidden from a king.

Since that birth, babies and kings and everybody else look different to us now — as in the poignant list of David Bentley Hart: " the autistic or Down syndrome or otherwise disabled child ... the derelict or wretched or broken man or woman who has wasted his or her life away; the homeless, the utterly impoverished, the diseased, the mentally ill, the physically disabled; exiles, refugees, fugitives; even criminals and reprobates." These were viewed by our ancient ancestors as burdens to be discarded. To see them instead as bearers of divine glory who can touch our conscience and still our selfishness — this is what Jesus saw that Herod could not see.

Strange reversal. Men who wear purple robes and glittering crowns and gaudy titles begin to look ridiculous — (when is the last time a politician attached "the Great" to his name?) — and yet the figure of the child born in a manger seems only to grow in stature. "We see the glory of God in a crucified slave, and [consequently] ... we see the forsaken of the earth as the very children of heaven"

He came into the world with no dignity.

Sources

The Mother

9: *"Behold the Lord's servant"*: Luke 1:38 paraphrased.

9: *"My soul glorifies"*: Luke 1:46.

10: *"Without dismissing"*: Scot McKnight, *The Real Mary* (London: SPCK, 2007), 31.

12: *"Nothing is impossible"*: Luke 1:37 NLT.

12: *Great Inversion*: See, for example, Mark 10:31; Luke 13:30.

12: *"He has filled"*: Luke 1:53.

13: *"Not my will"*: Luke 22:42.

The Child

18: *"No one in Herod's period"*: Peter Richardson, *Herod: King of the Jews, Friend of the Romans* (Columbia: University of South Carolina Press, 1996), 12.

21: *"When King Herod heard this"*: Matthew 2:3.

21: *"Was furious, and he gave orders"*: Matthew 2:16 – 18.

22: *"O Little Town of Bethlehem"*: Words by Phillips Brooks, music by Lewis H. Redner.

23: *"Rachel weeping for her children"*: Matthew 2:18.

23: *"Go and search carefully"*: Matthew 2:8, 9, 11, 13, 19.

24: Plato and Pliny the Elder: Cited in O. M. Bakke, *When Children Became People:*

The Birth of Childhood in Early Christianity (Minneapolis: Augsburg Fortress, 2005), 16–18.

25: "After Herod died": Matthew 2:19.

29: Aristotle, Politics, bk. 1, chap. 5.

29: Nicholas Wolterstorff, Justice: Rights and Wrongs (Princeton, NJ: Princeton University Press, 2008).

30: Martin Luther King Jr.: Source unknown.

33: Plutarch: Quoted in Bakke, When Children Became People, 30.

33: "Kopros": W. V. Harris, "Child Exposure in the Roman Empire," in Journal of Roman Studies 84 (1994): 1–22.

34: "A gruesome discovery": Bakke, When Children Became People, 32.

34: "Who . . . is the greatest": Matthew 18:1–4.

35: "An example of conversion": See Frederick Dale Bruner, Matthew: A Commentary, vol. 2, The Churchbook (Grand Rapids: Eerdmans, 2004), 209.

35: "And whoever welcomes": Matthew 18:5.

36: "Let the little children": Matthew 19:14.

36: Shepherd of Hermas: Quoted in Bakke, When Children Became People, 66.

37: G. K. Chesterton, The Everlasting Man (New York: Dodd Mead, 1930), 243–44.

42: David Bentley Hart, Atheist Delusions: The Christian Revolution and Its Fashionable Enemies (New Haven, CT: Yale University Press, 2009), 175.

43: "We see the glory of God": Ibid.

Who Is This Man?

The Unpredictable
Impact of the
Inescapable Jesus

John Ortberg

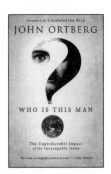

Jesus' impact on our world is highly unlikely, widely
inescapable, largely unknown, and decidedly
double-edged. He is history's most familiar figure,
yet he is the man no one knows. His impact on the
world is immense and non-accidental. From the
Dark Ages to Postmodernity he is the Man who
won't go away.

And yet ... you can miss him for many reasons,
maybe the most obvious being the way he lived
his life. He did not loudly defend his movement
in the spirit of a rising political or military leader.
He made history by starting in a humble place, in
a spirit of love and acceptance, and allowing each
person space to respond.

His vision of life continues to haunt and chal-
lenge humanity.

Share Your Thoughts

With the Author: Your comments will be forwarded to the author when you send them to *zauthor@zondervan.com*.

With Zondervan: Submit your review of this book by writing to *zreview@zondervan.com*.

Free Online Resources at
www.zondervan.com

Zondervan AuthorTracker: Be notified whenever your favorite authors publish new books, go on tour, or post an update about what's happening in their lives at www.zondervan.com/authortracker.

Daily Bible Verses and Devotions: Enrich your life with daily Bible verses or devotions that help you start every morning focused on God. Visit www.zondervan.com/newsletters.

Free Email Publications: Sign up for newsletters on Christian living, academic resources, church ministry, fiction, children's resources, and more. Visit www.zondervan.com/newsletters.

Zondervan Bible Search: Find and compare Bible passages in a variety of translations at www.zondervanbiblesearch.com.

Other Benefits: Register to receive online benefits like coupons and special offers, or to participate in research.

ZONDERVAN®

ZONDERVAN.com/
AUTHORTRACKER
follow your favorite authors